# Social Media Marketing For Small Businesses

# Social Media Marketing For Small Businesses

## A step-by-step guide

Dakota Smith

ISBN: 9798393427184

# Dedication

To my family and friends who have supported and encouraged me throughout my journey, thank you for always believing in me. To the mentors and colleagues who have challenged me to grow and develop my skills, I am grateful for your guidance and wisdom.

And to all the failures, setbacks, and challenges that have tested my resolve and pushed me to persevere, thank you for the lessons you have taught me. Without your guidance, I would not be the person I am today, and I would not have been able to write this book.

This dedication is a tribute to all those who have played a role in shaping my journey, and a reminder that success is a collaborative effort that requires both support and resilience. Thank you for being a part of my journey, and I hope this book can be a source of inspiration and guidance for all those seeking to build a successful social media presence for their small businesses.

# Table Of Contents

# Introduction

In today's digital age, having a strong social media presence is no longer a luxury but a necessity for businesses of all sizes. With billions of users worldwide, social media platforms offer an unparalleled opportunity for small businesses to connect with their target audience, build brand awareness, and ultimately drive sales. However, navigating the ever-changing landscape of social media can be a daunting task for small business owners who often wear multiple hats and have limited time and resources.

This book, "Social Media Marketing for Small Businesses: A Step-by-Step Guide," is specifically designed to help you, the small business owner, unlock the potential of social media marketing without feeling overwhelmed. We will walk you through the process of choosing the right platforms, developing a consistent brand voice and identity, creating engaging content, building your audience, and tracking your performance. Moreover, this guide is tailored to address the unique challenges faced by small businesses in the digital marketing landscape, with a focus on cost-effective and efficient strategies.

The importance of social media for small businesses cannot be overstated. According to recent statistics, more than half of the world's population uses social media, and users spend an average of 2 hours and 25 minutes per day on social platforms. Furthermore, 90% of users follow at least one business on social media, and 43% of internet users research products online through social networks. This presents an incredible opportunity for small businesses to tap into a vast and engaged audience.

However, with great opportunity comes great competition. There are millions of businesses vying for attention on social media, making it increasingly challenging to stand out and capture your target audience's attention. This is where a well-thought-out and executed social media marketing strategy comes into play. By following the step-by-step guidance provided in this book, you will be equipped with the tools and knowledge to create a winning social media strategy that sets your business apart from the competition.

# How to use this guide effectively

This book is designed to be both informative and practical, providing you with a solid foundation in social media marketing while offering actionable tips and strategies that you can apply to your business immediately. To get the most out of this guide, we recommend the following approach:

1. Read through the entire book to gain a comprehensive understanding of the social media marketing process and the various strategies available to you.

2. Revisit each chapter and take notes on the specific steps and tips that are most relevant to your business and goals.

3. Create an action plan based on the information and strategies provided in this guide, and start implementing it in your business.

4. Periodically review your progress and make adjustments to your strategy as needed. Social media is a constantly evolving landscape, and it's crucial to stay agile and adapt to new trends and best practices.

Remember, social media marketing is an ongoing process that requires patience, persistence, and consistent effort. By following the guidance provided in this book and staying committed to your social media strategy, you will be well on your way to achieving social media success and growing your small business.

Get ready to embark on your social media marketing journey and unlock the power of social media for your small business. Let's dive in!

# Chapter 1: Choosing the Right Social Media Platforms

As a small business owner venturing into the world of social media marketing, one of the first and most crucial decisions you'll need to make is choosing the right social media platforms to focus your efforts on. With a plethora of social media platforms available, each with its own unique features, user demographics, and content formats, it's essential to select the platforms that align best with your business goals, target audience, and the type of content you plan to create.

# Overview of Popular Social Media Platforms

Let's start by providing a brief overview of some of the most popular social media platforms today:

1. Facebook: With over 2.8 billion monthly active users, Facebook is the largest social media platform globally. Its diverse user base makes it a great platform for businesses of all types and sizes. Facebook allows businesses to create a dedicated page, post various types of content, interact with their audience, and run targeted ads.

2. Instagram: Instagram is a visually focused platform that's popular among younger demographics, particularly those under 35. It's an excellent platform for businesses that can produce high-quality photos and videos, such as fashion, food, and lifestyle brands.

3. Twitter: Twitter is a real-time communication platform where users share short messages called tweets. It's a great platform for businesses to share timely updates, engage in conversations, and provide customer service.

4. LinkedIn: LinkedIn is a professional networking platform that's ideal for B2B companies, service

providers, and businesses looking to recruit employees. It's a great place to share industry news, company updates, and thought leadership content.

5. Pinterest: Pinterest is a visual discovery platform where users find and save ideas and inspiration, often in the form of images linked to products or content. It's highly effective for businesses in the home decor, fashion, food, and DIY sectors.

6. TikTok: TikTok is a short-form video platform that's exploded in popularity, especially among Gen Z users. It's an excellent platform for businesses capable of creating entertaining, engaging video content.

7. Snapchat: Snapchat is a platform for sharing short-lived photos and videos, known for its younger user base. It can be a good platform for businesses looking to reach a younger audience with creative and fun content.

# Identifying Your Target Audience

To choose the right social media platforms for your business, you first need to understand your target audience. Who are they? What are their demographics (age, gender, location, etc.)? What are their interests and behaviors? Which social media platforms do they use most frequently?

Conducting audience research can help you answer these questions. You can gather this information through customer surveys, feedback, and online research. Social media platforms also provide demographic data about their users, which can be a valuable resource.

# Selecting the Most Suitable Platforms for Your Business

Once you've identified your target audience and their preferred social media platforms, it's time to select the platforms that align best with your business. Consider the following factors:

1. Audience match: Choose the platforms where your target audience spends most of their time.

2. Content match: Consider the type of content you plan to create and choose the platforms that support that content format. For example, if you plan to create a lot of video content, platforms like Instagram and TikTok might be a good fit.

3. Resources: Managing a social media platform takes time and effort, so consider your resources. It's better to manage one or two

platforms well than to spread yourself too thin across multiple platforms.

Choosing the right social media platforms is a crucial first step in your social media marketing journey. By understanding the different platforms, identifying your target

---

# Case Study: Understanding Your Audience

Jane, a talented jewelry maker, wanted to build a strong social media presence for her handmade jewelry business. She realized that to create a successful social media strategy, she needed to understand her target audience thoroughly. Jane began by conducting market research, including online surveys, analyzing her competitors' followers, and reviewing industry trends.

Based on her research, Jane created detailed buyer personas representing her ideal customers. These personas included information about their demographics, interests, and online behaviors. Jane discovered that her target audience was primarily composed of environmentally conscious women who valued unique, handcrafted, and ethically sourced jewelry.

With these insights, Jane tailored her social media strategy to appeal to her target audience's values and preferences. She focused on creating content that showcased her sustainable sourcing practices and shared behind-the-scenes stories of her jewelry-making process. Jane also highlighted the uniqueness of each piece, appealing to her audience's desire for individuality.

In addition, Jane began offering exclusive promotions and discounts to her social media followers, such as limited-time offers and special giveaways. This encouraged her audience to follow her closely and engage with her content, further strengthening their loyalty to her brand.

Over time, Jane's focused social media strategy, grounded in her understanding of her target audience, led to a significant increase in followers, engagement, and ultimately, sales. By consistently catering to her audience's needs and preferences, Jane successfully transformed her social media presence from a mere online showcase into a thriving community of passionate supporters.

# Chapter 2: Setting Your Social Media Objectives

A well-defined social media strategy begins with clear and measurable objectives. Establishing your social media objectives will help you stay focused on your goals, make informed decisions, and measure your progress over time. In this chapter, we'll discuss the importance of setting social media objectives, provide examples of objectives for small businesses, and guide you through aligning your objectives with your overall business goals.

# Importance of Setting Clear and Measurable Goals

Setting clear and measurable goals for your social media efforts is essential for several reasons:

1. Focus: Goals help you maintain focus on what matters most to your business, ensuring that your efforts and resources are directed towards achieving those outcomes.

2. Decision-making: Clear objectives act as a guide when making decisions about content, platform selection, and resource allocation.

3. Measurement: Measurable goals allow you to track your progress, identify areas for improvement, and evaluate the overall effectiveness of your social media strategy.

# Examples of Social Media Objectives for Small Businesses

While your specific objectives will depend on your business goals and industry, here are some common social media objectives that small businesses often aim to achieve:

1. Brand awareness: Increase visibility and recognition for your brand, products, or services.
2. Community building: Grow and engage with your target audience, fostering a sense of community and loyalty among your followers.
3. Lead generation: Attract potential customers and collect their contact information for further nurturing and conversion.
4. Customer service: Provide timely and effective support to your customers, addressing their questions, concerns, and feedback.
5. Website traffic: Drive visitors from your social media profiles to your website or online store.
6. Sales: Increase revenue through direct product promotion, special offers, and advertising.

When setting your social media objectives, make sure they are SMART: Specific, Measurable, Achievable, Relevant, and Time-bound.

# Aligning Your Objectives with Your Overall Business Goals

To ensure that your social media efforts contribute to your overall business success, it's essential to align your social media objectives with your broader business goals. Consider how your social media efforts can support your business's marketing, sales, customer service, and brand-building goals.

For example, if one of your primary business goals is to increase sales by 20% in the next year, your social media objectives might include increasing brand awareness, driving traffic to your online store, and promoting special offers to drive sales. By aligning your social media objectives with your business goals, you can ensure that your efforts are focused on driving tangible results for your business.

Setting clear and measurable social media objectives is a crucial step in creating an effective social media marketing strategy. By establishing your goals upfront and aligning them with your overall business objectives, you can ensure that your social media efforts stay focused, informed, and results-driven. In the next chapter, we'll dive into developing your brand voice and identity, which will lay the foundation for your social media content and engagement strategies.

---

# Case Study: Setting Clear Objectives

Pete, a personal trainer, decided to use social media to grow his fitness studio and reach a wider audience. However, he realized that without clear objectives, it would be difficult to focus his efforts and measure the success of his social media strategy. Pete decided to attend a social media marketing workshop to learn about best practices for setting goals and measuring results.

After the workshop, Pete began by setting clear, measurable, and achievable objectives for his social media efforts. These objectives included increasing his followers by 20% in three months, boosting engagement on his posts by 15%, and converting 5% of his online interactions into trial memberships at his studio. He also set a goal to improve his studio's online reputation by consistently receiving positive reviews from satisfied clients.

With these objectives in place, Pete developed a targeted social media strategy that focused on showcasing his fitness studio's unique offerings, sharing success stories from his clients, and providing valuable fitness tips and advice. He also began hosting live workout sessions and Q&A sessions to engage with his followers and build a sense of community around his fitness studio.

To measure the effectiveness of his social media strategy, Pete utilized various analytics tools to track his progress against his objectives. This allowed him to identify which tactics were working and which ones needed adjustments. For instance, Pete discovered that his live workout sessions were attracting a significant number of new followers, while his Q&A sessions were driving higher engagement rates.

As Pete continued to refine his social media strategy based on his objectives and the data he collected, he saw significant improvements in his online presence. Not only did he achieve his goals of increasing followers and engagement, but he also successfully converted a portion of his online audience into trial memberships at his fitness studio. By setting clear objectives and consistently measuring his progress, Pete was able to create a focused and effective social media strategy that contributed to the growth of his fitness studio.

# Chapter 3: Developing Your Brand Voice and Identity

To stand out on social media and resonate with your target audience, it's crucial to develop a consistent brand voice and identity. Your brand voice represents the personality and tone of your business, while your visual identity encompasses the visual elements that make your brand unique, such as colors, fonts, and imagery. In this chapter, we'll explore how to define your brand voice, create a consistent visual identity, and provide tips for crafting engaging content.

# Defining Your Brand Voice

Your brand voice is the way your business communicates with your audience through written and spoken words. It should be consistent across all your marketing channels, including social media, to create a cohesive and recognizable brand experience. To define your brand voice, consider the following steps:

1. Understand your target audience: Your brand voice should resonate with your target audience. Consider their demographics, interests, and preferences when crafting your brand voice.

2. Reflect on your business values: Your brand voice should align with your company's values, mission, and vision. Think about what makes your business unique and how you want to communicate that to your audience.

3. Choose your brand voice attributes: Identify three to five adjectives that best describe your brand voice. Examples include professional, friendly, informative, playful, or conversational. These attributes will guide your tone and style in all your social media content.

4. Create a brand voice guide: Document your brand voice attributes, along with examples and guidelines for how to apply them in your social

media content. This will help ensure consistency across your team and content creators.

# Creating a Consistent Visual Identity

A strong visual identity helps your brand stand out and be easily recognized on social media. To create a consistent visual identity, consider the following elements:

1. Logo: Your logo is a key visual element that represents your brand. Make sure it's consistently used across all your social media profiles and content.

2. Color palette: Choose a color palette that reflects your brand's personality and is consistent with your other marketing materials. Use these colors consistently in your social media content.

3. Typography: Select one or two fonts that align with your brand voice and use them consistently across your social media content.

4. Imagery: Use consistent imagery that aligns with your brand's visual identity and communicates your message effectively. This may include photographs, illustrations, icons, and graphics.

5.  Templates: Create templates for your social media content to ensure consistency in layout, design, and style.

# Tips for Crafting Engaging Content

With your brand voice and visual identity established, you're ready to start creating engaging social media content. Here are some tips to help you craft content that resonates with your audience:

1.  Know your audience: Understand your target audience's preferences and tailor your content to their interests and needs.

2.  Tell a story: Share stories that humanize your brand, highlight customer success stories, or showcase the people behind your business.

3.  Be authentic: Be genuine and transparent in your communication. Avoid overly promotional or sales-driven content.

4.  Encourage engagement: Create content that encourages your audience to like, comment, share, and interact with your brand. Ask questions, run polls, or host giveaways to boost engagement.

5. Monitor trends: Stay up-to-date with industry trends, news, and popular culture to create relevant and timely content.

Developing a consistent brand voice and visual identity is essential for creating a strong and memorable social media presence. By following the guidelines outlined in this chapter, you'll be well-equipped to craft engaging content that resonates with your target audience and builds brand recognition. In the next chapter, we'll delve into creating a social media content

---

# Case Study: Creating Engaging Content

Amy, the owner of a vegan bakery, wanted to promote her business on social media and create a strong online presence. She understood that simply posting promotional content wouldn't be enough to attract and retain a loyal following. Amy knew that she needed to create a variety of engaging content that would appeal to her target audience of vegan food enthusiasts and showcase the unique aspects of her bakery.

To start, Amy researched the interests and preferences of her target audience. She discovered that they were not only interested in delicious vegan treats but also wanted to learn more about the benefits of a vegan lifestyle, the ingredients used in her products, and the ethical practices behind her business. With this information, Amy began brainstorming content ideas that would address her audience's desires while also highlighting her bakery's offerings.

Amy decided to create a content calendar to ensure she consistently published diverse and engaging content. She committed to posting mouth-watering images of her products, accompanied by enticing captions and relevant hashtags to attract potential customers. Amy also began sharing recipe tutorials, providing her audience with valuable insights into creating delicious vegan treats at home. This helped establish Amy as an authority in the vegan baking space and fostered a sense of trust among her followers.

To further engage her audience, Amy started sharing behind-the-scenes glimpses into her bakery, including the process of making her treats, the team members who brought her creations to life, and the care taken to source high-quality, ethically-sourced ingredients. These posts helped humanize her brand and forge a personal connection with her followers.

Amy also made an effort to interact with her audience by responding to their comments, answering their questions, and encouraging them to share their own experiences with her products. This not only increased engagement on her posts but also helped her to build a community of loyal fans who felt seen and appreciated.

As Amy continued to publish engaging content that resonated with her audience, she noticed a significant increase in her social media following, engagement rates, and ultimately, sales at her bakery. By consistently delivering valuable and engaging content, Amy successfully attracted a large and engaged audience of vegan food enthusiasts who became dedicated customers and advocates for her business.

# Chapter 4: Creating a Social Media Content Strategy

With a well-defined brand voice and visual identity in place, it's time to create a social media content plan that will guide your efforts and keep you organized. A content plan outlines the types of content you'll create, the frequency of posting, and the distribution across your chosen platforms. In this chapter, we'll discuss the steps to create a social media content plan, provide tips on content creation, and explore tools to help you stay organized and consistent.

# Steps to Create a Social Media Content Plan

1. Determine content types: Based on your brand voice, visual identity, and social media objectives, identify the types of content you want to create. This may include blog post shares, product promotions, behind-the-scenes glimpses, customer testimonials, or educational content.

2. Establish a posting frequency: Decide how often you'll post content on each social media platform. Keep in mind that the ideal posting frequency will vary depending on the platform and your audience's preferences. Start with a manageable schedule and adjust as needed based on your results and audience engagement.

3. Create a content calendar: Develop a content calendar that outlines your planned content for each platform, including posting dates, times, and any relevant details. This will help you stay organized and ensure you have a consistent content mix across your platforms.

4. Allocate resources: Identify the team members responsible for creating, approving, and posting

your social media content. Ensure they have the necessary tools and resources to execute your content plan effectively.

5. Monitor and adjust: Regularly review your content plan and performance to identify areas for improvement. Adjust your content types, posting frequency, and distribution based on your findings.

# Tips for Content Creation

1. Batch content creation: To streamline your content creation process, consider creating content in batches. This allows you to focus on one type of content at a time, improving efficiency and consistency.

2. Repurpose content: Maximize the value of your existing content by repurposing it for different platforms and formats. For example, turn a blog post into a series of social media graphics or an infographic into a short video.

3. Curate content: Supplement your original content with curated content from other sources that your audience will find valuable. This can help position your brand as a thought leader and save time on content creation.

4. Collaborate: Involve your team, customers, and partners in your content creation process. This can provide fresh perspectives, increase engagement, and create a sense of community around your brand.

# Tools for Content Planning and Organization

To help you stay organized and execute your content plan effectively, consider using the following tools:

1. Content calendars: Tools like Google Calendar, Trello, or Asana can help you create and manage your content calendar, assign tasks, and track progress.
2. Social media management tools: Platforms like Hootsuite, Buffer, or Sprout Social allow you to schedule and publish content across multiple social media platforms, monitor engagement, and analyze performance.
3. Design tools: Use design tools like Canva, Adobe Spark, or Crello to create visually appealing and on-brand social media graphics and visuals.

A well-structured social media content plan is essential for staying organized, consistent, and focused on your social media objectives. By following the steps outlined in this chapter and leveraging the tips and tools provided, you'll be well-equipped to create engaging content that resonates with your audience and drives results for your business. In the next chapter, we'll explore strategies for growing your audience and building a loyal community around your brand.

---

# Case Study: Leveraging Hashtags, Influencers, and Partnerships

John, the owner of an outdoor gear store, wanted to expand his social media reach and attract a larger, more engaged audience interested in outdoor activities. He knew that to achieve this, he needed to implement a multi-faceted social media strategy that went beyond just posting about his products. John decided to focus on leveraging hashtags, influencers, and partnerships to amplify his message and extend his reach to a broader audience.

To begin, John researched popular and relevant hashtags within the outdoor community. He identified a mix of general hashtags, such as #outdoorlife and #adventure, as well as niche hashtags specific to various outdoor activities, like #hiking, #camping, and #backpacking. By incorporating these hashtags into his posts, John was able to increase the visibility of his content and attract new followers who shared his passion for the outdoors.

Next, John sought out partnerships with influencers in the outdoor community. He identified individuals who were not only passionate about outdoor activities but also had a strong online following and a high level of engagement with their audience. John reached out to these influencers and offered them exclusive discounts, free products, or sponsored content opportunities in exchange for promoting his store and products on their social media channels.

These partnerships helped John tap into a larger audience that was already interested in outdoor activities and positioned his store as a trusted source for high-quality gear. In addition to influencers, John looked for opportunities to collaborate with complementary businesses in the outdoor space. He partnered with local outdoor adventure tour companies, camping grounds, and even a nearby eco-lodge to create co-branded content and promotions. For example, John's store and a local camping ground might jointly host a giveaway contest, where participants could win a camping package that included gear from John's store and a weekend stay at the camping ground. These collaborations allowed John to expand his reach further and introduce his store to new potential customers who were already engaged in outdoor activities.

Throughout his social media campaigns, John made sure to track the performance of his partnerships, hashtags, and collaborations. By analyzing the data, he was able to determine which tactics were most effective in driving engagement, followers, and sales, and he adjusted his strategy accordingly.

As a result of his efforts in leveraging hashtags, influencers, and partnerships, John was able to significantly extend his social media reach and attract a larger, more engaged audience. Not only did his online presence grow, but he also saw a positive impact on his store's sales and overall brand reputation.

# Chapter 5: Best Practices for Each Social Media Platform

A successful social media presence relies on a strong and engaged audience. By growing your audience and fostering a sense of community, you'll create a loyal customer base that will support and advocate for your brand. In this chapter, we'll discuss strategies to attract new followers, increase engagement, and build a loyal community around your brand.

# Attracting New Followers

1. Optimize your profiles: Ensure your social media profiles are complete, on-brand, and optimized with relevant keywords and hashtags. This will improve your visibility in platform searches and make it easier for potential followers to find you.

2. Promote your social media channels: Share your social media profiles on your website, email signatures, business cards, and other marketing materials to encourage your existing customers and contacts to follow you.

3. Collaborate with influencers: Partner with influencers in your industry to expand your reach and credibility. Influencers can introduce your brand to their audience through sponsored posts, product reviews, or collaborations.

4. Participate in relevant conversations: Engage with your target audience by participating in relevant conversations, groups, or communities. Share valuable insights, answer questions, and provide support to demonstrate your expertise and attract new followers.

5. Run targeted ads: Utilize social media advertising to reach your target audience and promote your content, products, or services. Use

platform targeting features to ensure your ads are shown to users who are likely to be interested in your brand.

# Increasing Engagement

1. Create valuable content: Publish content that is informative, entertaining, or inspiring to encourage likes, comments, and shares. High-quality content that resonates with your audience is more likely to be shared and engaged with.

2. Ask questions and encourage feedback: Encourage your audience to share their thoughts and opinions by asking questions, running polls, or requesting feedback on your content, products, or services.

3. Respond to comments and messages: Show your audience that you value their input by responding to their comments and messages in a timely manner. Engaging with your audience helps to build rapport and encourages future interactions.

4. Host giveaways and contests: Run giveaways or contests that require users to like, comment, or share your content to enter. This can increase engagement and attract new followers.

5. Share user-generated content: Share content created by your followers, such as testimonials, photos, or videos featuring your products or services. This not only increases engagement but also helps to build trust and credibility with your audience.

# Building a Loyal Community

1. Showcase your brand personality: Humanize your brand by sharing behind-the-scenes content, featuring team members, or telling stories about your company's history and values.

2. Celebrate milestones and achievements: Share your successes and milestones with your audience to create a sense of shared achievement and foster a sense of community.

3. Support causes and initiatives: Align your brand with causes or initiatives that resonate with your audience and reflect your company values. This can help you connect with your audience on a deeper level and build brand loyalty.

4. Create a branded hashtag: Encourage your audience to share content related to your brand by creating a branded hashtag. This will make it easier for your followers to find and engage with content related to your brand.

5. Host events or meetups: Organize events, meetups, or online gatherings where your followers can connect with you and each other. This can help strengthen your community and foster a sense of belonging among your audience.

Growing your audience and building a loyal community is crucial for establishing a strong and sustainable social media presence. By implementing the strategies outlined in this chapter, you can attract new followers, increase engagement,

---

# Case Study: Boosting Engagement with Contests and Giveaways

Sarah, a boutique owner, wanted to boost her social media engagement and create excitement around her brand. After researching various tactics, she decided that contests and giveaways would be an effective way to achieve her goals. Sarah understood that these types of promotions could not only increase engagement on her posts but also attract new followers and generate buzz around her brand.

To start, Sarah outlined a strategy for her contests and giveaways. She decided to host a variety of promotions, including weekly giveaways, seasonal contests, and milestone celebrations. Sarah wanted to ensure that her promotions were engaging and offered her followers a genuine opportunity to win exclusive prizes that showcased her boutique's unique offerings.

For her weekly giveaways, Sarah selected a popular item from her boutique, such as a trendy handbag or fashionable accessory, and encouraged her followers to participate by liking, sharing, and commenting on her posts. She also asked them to tag friends who might be interested in the giveaway, further expanding her boutique's reach. These weekly giveaways not only increased engagement on her posts but also provided her followers with a sense of anticipation and excitement as they looked forward to the next giveaway.

In addition to her weekly promotions, Sarah hosted seasonal contests that aligned with major fashion events or holidays. For example, during Fashion Week, she invited her followers to submit photos of their most stylish outfits using a branded hashtag. The winning participant would receive a gift card to her boutique. This contest not only encouraged user-generated content but also showcased the creativity and style of her followers, further reinforcing her brand's reputation as a go-to destination for fashion-forward individuals.

Lastly, Sarah celebrated major milestones, such as reaching a specific number of followers or her boutique's anniversary, with special giveaways or promotions. These celebrations not only recognized her loyal followers but also helped to create a sense of community and belonging around her brand.

Throughout her promotional campaigns, Sarah made sure to monitor the performance of her contests and giveaways. She tracked key metrics, such as engagement, follower growth, and website traffic, to determine which promotions resonated most with her audience. Based on her analysis, Sarah refined her strategy to focus on the most successful tactics and continuously improve her promotions.

By offering her followers the chance to win exclusive prizes through contests and giveaways, Sarah not only increased engagement on her posts but also attracted new followers and generated buzz around her brand. As a result, her boutique experienced a boost in online visibility, brand awareness, and ultimately, sales.

# Chapter 6: Building Your Audience and Engagement

To ensure that your social media efforts are driving results and contributing to your overall business objectives, it's crucial to measure and analyze your performance regularly. By tracking key metrics, you can identify areas for improvement, optimize your content and strategies, and make data-driven decisions. In this chapter, we'll discuss the importance of social media analytics, explore key performance indicators (KPIs) for small businesses, and provide tips for analyzing and improving your social media performance.

# The Importance of Social Media Analytics

Social media analytics are essential for several reasons:

1. Understand your audience: Analytics provide insights into your audience's demographics, interests, and behaviors, helping you tailor your content and strategies accordingly.

2. Measure your progress: By tracking your performance over time, you can evaluate whether you're achieving your social media objectives and overall business goals.

3. Optimize your content: Analytics help you identify which types of content resonate most with your audience, enabling you to optimize your content plan and improve engagement.

4. Identify trends: Analyzing your performance data can help you spot trends, opportunities, and threats, allowing you to adapt your strategies and stay ahead of the competition.

# Key Performance Indicators (KPIs) for Small Businesses

While the specific KPIs you track will depend on your social media objectives and overall business goals, here are some common KPIs that small businesses often monitor:

1. Follower growth: The number of new followers you gain over time, indicating the success of your audience-building efforts.

2. Engagement: Metrics such as likes, comments, shares, and click-throughs that show how your audience is interacting with your content.

3. Reach and impressions: The number of people who see your content, indicating the visibility and potential impact of your social media efforts.

4. Website traffic: The number of visitors to your website or online store from your social media profiles, indicating the success of your efforts to drive traffic and generate leads.

5. Conversion rate: The percentage of your social media followers or website visitors who take a desired action, such as making a purchase, signing up for a newsletter, or requesting a quote.

# Tips for Analyzing and Improving Your Social Media Performance

1. Benchmark your performance: Compare your performance metrics against industry benchmarks or your past performance to identify areas for improvement and set realistic goals.

2. Conduct A/B tests: Experiment with different types of content, posting times, and platform features to identify what works best for your audience and optimize your strategies.

3. Monitor competitors: Keep an eye on your competitors' social media efforts to gain insights into their strategies, successes, and areas where you can differentiate yourself.

4. Leverage platform analytics tools: Utilize native analytics tools available on each social media platform, such as Facebook Insights, Instagram Insights, or Twitter Analytics, to gather detailed performance data and insights.

5. Use third-party analytics tools: Consider using third-party analytics tools like Hootsuite, Buffer, or Sprout Social to consolidate your data across platforms, conduct in-depth analysis, and automate reporting.

Measuring and analyzing your social media performance is critical for optimizing your efforts and driving results for your business. By tracking relevant KPIs, conducting regular analysis, and leveraging the tips and tools provided in this chapter, you can make informed decisions, improve your social media strategies, and achieve your objectives. In the next chapter, we'll explore advanced strategies and tactics to further elevate your social media presence and drive even greater results for your business.

---

# Case Study: Utilizing Paid Advertising

Tom, the owner of a tech shop, wanted to reach a larger audience on social media and drive more sales for his business. After considering various strategies, he decided to invest in paid advertising on platforms like Facebook and Instagram. Tom understood that by leveraging the advanced targeting capabilities of these platforms, he could reach a highly relevant audience of users interested in technology and electronics, thus increasing his chances of generating new leads and sales.

Before launching his paid advertising campaigns, Tom carefully researched his target audience, identifying their demographics, interests, and online behaviors. He wanted to ensure that his ads would be seen by users who were most likely to be interested in his products and services. With this information in hand, Tom began crafting his advertising strategy.

Tom decided to create a mix of advertising formats, including carousel ads showcasing multiple products, video ads demonstrating the features of popular gadgets, and dynamic product ads retargeting users who had previously visited his website. He also experimented with different ad placements, such as Instagram Stories, Facebook News Feed, and Audience Network, to maximize his reach and find the most effective placements for his target audience.

To optimize his campaigns, Tom tested various ad creatives and copy variations. He wanted to identify which combinations generated the highest engagement and conversion rates. By consistently monitoring the performance of his ads and making adjustments based on the data, Tom ensured that his campaigns remained effective and cost-efficient.

In addition to his regular ad campaigns, Tom took advantage of seasonal promotions and special events to create time-sensitive offers and limited-time deals.

These campaigns not only created a sense of urgency among his audience but also helped him capitalize on increased online shopping activity during peak seasons.

As Tom's paid advertising campaigns gained traction, he began to see a significant increase in his brand visibility and website traffic. He also noticed an uptick in new leads and sales, as more users discovered his tech shop through his targeted ads. Over time, Tom refined his advertising strategy, investing more in the platforms, ad formats, and targeting options that generated the best results for his business.

Through effective ad targeting, creative experimentation, and continuous optimization, Tom successfully increased his brand visibility and generated new leads for his tech shop. His investment in paid advertising not only helped him reach a larger audience on social media but also contributed to the growth and success of his business.

# Chapter 7: Paid Social Media Advertising for Small Businesses

As your social media presence grows and evolves, you may find yourself looking for advanced strategies and tactics to further boost your performance and drive greater results for your business. In this chapter, we'll explore several advanced techniques, including leveraging platform-specific features, using social listening tools, and employing retargeting campaigns, to help you take your social media efforts to the next level.

# Leveraging Platform-Specific Features

Each social media platform offers unique features and tools that can enhance your content and strategies. Here are some examples:

1. Instagram Stories and Reels: Use Instagram Stories and Reels to share short-lived, interactive content that complements your regular posts. This can help you showcase your brand personality, engage your audience, and increase your visibility in the platform's algorithm.

2. LinkedIn Showcase Pages: Create LinkedIn Showcase Pages to highlight specific products, services, or initiatives, and target relevant audiences. This can help you segment your content and engage more effectively with different customer segments.

3. Facebook Groups: Establish and manage a Facebook Group for your business to create a dedicated space for your community to connect, share, and engage with your brand and each other.

4. Twitter Spaces: Host live audio conversations using Twitter Spaces to connect with your audience, share insights, and facilitate

discussions on topics related to your industry or business.

# Using Social Listening Tools

1. Social listening tools can help you monitor online conversations about your brand, industry, and competitors, providing valuable insights to inform your social media strategies. Here are some benefits of using social listening tools:

2. Identify trends and opportunities: Stay ahead of the curve by identifying emerging trends, opportunities, and threats in your industry or market.

3. Monitor brand sentiment: Track and analyze public sentiment about your brand to identify areas for improvement, potential crises, and opportunities to delight your customers.

4. Analyze competitor performance: Gain insights into your competitors' social media strategies, successes, and weaknesses to inform your own approach.

5. Discover influencers and advocates: Identify influential users and brand advocates who can help amplify your message and strengthen your reputation.

6. Popular social listening tools include Brandwatch, Mention, and Awario, among others.

# Employing Retargeting Campaigns

1. Retargeting campaigns allow you to serve ads to users who have previously engaged with your brand or visited your website, increasing the likelihood of conversion. Here's how to implement retargeting campaigns on social media:

2. Install tracking pixels: Install tracking pixels, such as the Facebook Pixel or LinkedIn Insight Tag, on your website to gather data on your visitors and their behaviors.

3. Create custom audiences: Use your tracking pixel data to create custom audiences based on user behavior, such as website visits, product views, or abandoned carts.

4. Develop targeted ad campaigns: Design and launch retargeting ad campaigns on social media platforms, targeting your custom audiences with personalized messaging and offers.

5. Analyze and optimize: Monitor the performance of your retargeting campaigns and optimize your targeting, messaging, and budgets based on your results.

Implementing advanced strategies and tactics can help you further elevate your social media presence and drive greater results for your business. By leveraging platform-specific features, using social listening tools, and employing retargeting campaigns, you can stay ahead of the competition, engage your audience more effectively, and achieve your social media objectives. As you continue to grow and evolve your social media efforts, remember to stay flexible, adapt to new trends and technologies, and always keep your audience and business goals at the forefront of your strategy.

---

# Case Study: Measuring and Analyzing Performance

Mary, an art gallery owner, wanted to improve her social media efforts and maximize the return on her investment. She understood that in order to achieve this, she needed to regularly track her performance and make data-driven decisions. By using platform analytics and third-party tools, Mary began to analyze her engagement, follower growth, and other key metrics, which allowed her to identify areas for improvement, adjust her strategy, and achieve better results.

To start, Mary familiarized herself with the built-in analytics tools on her chosen social media platforms, such as Facebook Insights, Instagram Insights, and Twitter Analytics. She also explored third-party tools, like Hootsuite and Sprout Social, to gather additional data and gain deeper insights into her social media performance. By combining these resources, Mary was able to develop a comprehensive understanding of how her content and campaigns were resonating with her audience.

Mary created a custom dashboard to track her key performance indicators (KPIs), such as engagement rate, follower growth, reach, impressions, and conversions. She also monitored more granular metrics, like the best time to post, top-performing content, and audience demographics. By regularly reviewing these metrics, Mary was able to pinpoint trends, patterns, and areas for improvement in her social media strategy.

One key insight Mary discovered was that her audience engaged more with behind-the-scenes content and artist interviews than with promotional posts about upcoming exhibitions. Armed with this information, Mary adjusted her content strategy to focus more on human-interest stories and interactive content, which led to increased engagement and a more loyal following. Another valuable finding was that certain types of posts, such as limited-time promotions and flash sales, drove a higher number of conversions than others. Mary leveraged this insight to create more targeted and timely offers for her audience, resulting in a boost in online sales and gallery visits.

Mary also found that her follower growth had plateaued, prompting her to explore new tactics to expand her reach. She experimented with paid advertising, influencer partnerships, and cross-promotions with complementary businesses, which helped her reach new audiences and revive her follower growth.

As Mary continued to measure and analyze her performance, she became more adept at identifying opportunities and adjusting her strategy accordingly. She regularly tested new tactics, content types, and targeting options, always seeking to optimize her social media efforts and achieve better results.

By consistently tracking her performance using platform analytics and third-party tools, Mary was able to make informed decisions, refine her social media strategy, and ultimately, achieve greater success for her art gallery. Her commitment to data-driven decision-making not only improved her online presence but also contributed to the growth and prosperity of her gallery.

# Chapter 8: Monitoring Your Social Media Performance

As the world of social media continues to evolve rapidly, it's essential to adapt your strategy to stay relevant and effective in the ever-changing landscape. In this chapter, we'll discuss the importance of staying agile, exploring emerging platforms and technologies, and continuously learning and refining your approach to future-proof your social media strategy.

# Staying Agile in a Changing Landscape

Monitor trends and developments: Regularly research and stay informed about the latest trends, platform updates, and industry news to ensure your strategy remains current and effective.

1. Embrace change and experimentation: Be open to change and willing to experiment with new platforms, features, and tactics. Not every experiment will be successful, but those that are can give you a competitive edge.

2. Continuously evaluate and adjust: Regularly assess the performance of your social media efforts and be prepared to make adjustments to your strategy based on the results and changing circumstances.

# Exploring Emerging Platforms and Technologies

1. Identify new opportunities: Keep an eye out for emerging platforms and technologies that may present new opportunities for your business. Consider whether they align with your audience

and objectives before investing time and resources.

2. Test and learn: Dip your toes into new platforms and technologies by running small-scale tests and learning from the results. This will help you determine whether a new platform or technology is worth incorporating into your strategy.

3. Balance innovation with consistency: While it's important to explore new opportunities, don't lose sight of the platforms and tactics that have proven effective for your business. Strive for a balance between innovation and consistency in your strategy.

# Continuous Learning and Refinement

1. Stay educated: Invest time in your own professional development by attending industry events, webinars, and conferences, and by reading articles, blogs, and books on social media marketing.

2. Network with industry professionals: Connect with other social media professionals to share experiences, insights, and best practices. Networking can help you stay informed, gain

fresh perspectives, and broaden your knowledge.

3. Seek feedback from your audience: Regularly solicit feedback from your followers and customers to gain valuable insights into what's working and what could be improved in your social media efforts.

4. Monitor your competitors: Keep an eye on your competitors' social media strategies and performance to gain insights, identify gaps, and stay ahead of the curve.

Adapting to the changing social media landscape and future-proofing your strategy is vital for long-term success. By staying agile, exploring emerging platforms and technologies, and continuously learning and refining your approach, you can ensure that your social media efforts remain relevant, effective, and aligned with your business goals. As you continue to navigate the world of social media, remember that your audience is at the heart of your strategy, and always strive to deliver value, build relationships, and drive results for your business.

# Case Study: Adapting to Changing Landscapes

David, a travel blogger, had built a substantial following on social media platforms like Facebook, Instagram, and Twitter. However, he noticed a decline in his social media engagement due to changing platform algorithms, trends, and user preferences. David understood that to maintain his social media relevance and continue growing his audience, he needed to adapt to the evolving digital landscape. He decided to research emerging platforms, test new content formats, and adjust his strategy accordingly. By staying agile and embracing change, David was able to keep his travel blog thriving and his audience engaged.

First, David conducted extensive research to stay up-to-date on the latest social media trends and platform updates. He subscribed to industry newsletters, followed influential social media experts, and participated in online forums and communities. This allowed him to gain insights into new platforms, content formats, and strategies that could potentially benefit his travel blog.

Based on his research, David identified several emerging platforms, such as TikTok and Clubhouse, that were gaining traction among his target audience. He decided to create accounts on these platforms and experiment with their unique content formats, such as short-form videos and live audio discussions. By diversifying his presence across multiple platforms, David was able to reach new audiences and tap into different user behaviors.David also discovered that certain content formats, like live streaming and user-generated content, were gaining popularity among his followers. He began incorporating these formats into his content strategy, hosting live Q&A sessions on Instagram, and encouraging his audience to share their own travel experiences using a branded hashtag. By adapting his content strategy to align with current trends, David was able to re-engage his audience and boost his social media engagement.

In addition to testing new platforms and content formats, David recognized the importance of monitoring the performance of his social media efforts. He regularly analyzed his engagement, reach, and other key metrics to determine which strategies were most effective and which needed to be adjusted. By closely tracking his performance and making data-driven decisions, David was able to continually refine his social media strategy and adapt to the ever-changing landscape.

As part of his commitment to staying agile, David also invested time in learning about new tools and technologies that could help him manage and optimize his social media efforts. He experimented with scheduling tools, analytics software, and content creation apps, always seeking to improve his workflow and enhance his online presence.

By actively researching, experimenting, and adapting to the changing social media landscape, David was able to maintain his relevance and continue to grow his audience. His dedication to staying agile and embracing change not only helped him overcome the challenges posed by evolving platform algorithms and trends but also positioned his travel blog for long-term success in the competitive digital space.

# Chapter 9: Time Management and Automation

As your social media presence and business grow, it's essential to scale your social media efforts to maintain momentum and continue driving results. In this chapter, we'll discuss strategies for scaling your social media efforts, including creating a content calendar, automating processes, and building a team to support your long-term growth.

# Creating a Content Calendar

A content calendar can help you plan, organize, and schedule your social media content in advance, ensuring consistency and efficiency in your efforts. Here are some tips for creating a content calendar:

1. Set content themes: Establish content themes that align with your business goals, audience interests, and social media objectives. This will help you maintain focus and deliver value to your audience.

2. Plan content in advance: Plan your content several weeks or even months in advance to ensure consistency, account for holidays and special events, and reduce stress.

3. Schedule content: Schedule your content using a tool like Hootsuite, Buffer, or Later to save time and ensure your content is published at optimal times for your audience.

4. Review and adjust: Regularly review your content calendar and make adjustments based on your performance, audience feedback, and emerging trends or opportunities.

# Automating Processes

Automating certain aspects of your social media efforts can help you save time, reduce manual work, and scale your efforts more efficiently. Here are some areas to consider for automation:

1. Content scheduling: Use scheduling tools to automate the posting of your content across multiple platforms and at optimal times.

2. Social media monitoring: Utilize social listening tools to automate the tracking of mentions, keywords, and hashtags relevant to your brand or industry.

3. Analytics and reporting: Leverage tools that automatically generate reports and insights on your social media performance, enabling you to make data-driven decisions more efficiently.

4. Customer service: Consider using chatbots or automated responses to assist with frequently asked questions and basic customer inquiries on your social media profiles.

# Building a Team

As your social media efforts grow, you may need to build a team to support your long-term growth and ensure consistent, high-quality content and engagement. Here are some tips for building your social media team:

1. Define roles and responsibilities: Clearly outline the roles and responsibilities of each team member, including content creation, community management, and analytics.

2. Hire the right talent: Look for individuals with the skills, experience, and passion for social media that align with your brand values and objectives.

3. Invest in training: Provide ongoing training and professional development opportunities to help your team stay current with industry trends, best practices, and platform updates.

4. Establish clear communication: Implement regular team meetings, updates, and communication channels to ensure everyone is aligned and working together effectively.

Scaling your social media efforts is crucial for long-term growth and success. By creating a content calendar, automating processes, and building a team to support your efforts, you can maintain momentum, drive results, and achieve your social media objectives. As you continue to grow, remember to stay adaptable, keep learning, and always focus on delivering value to your audience and supporting your business goals.

# Case Study: Scaling Social Media Efforts

Lisa, an online course creator, had experienced significant growth in her business and realized she needed to scale her social media efforts to keep up with the increasing demand. As her audience grew larger and her course offerings expanded, managing her social media presence became more complex and time-consuming. To maintain momentum and continue driving results, Lisa focused on implementing a content calendar, automating processes like content scheduling, and building a social media team to support her efforts. By scaling her social media efforts efficiently, Lisa was able to effectively manage her growing business while continuing to engage her audience and drive sales.

To begin, Lisa developed a content calendar to streamline her content creation process and ensure consistency across her social media channels. By planning her content in advance and organizing it in a visual calendar format, Lisa was able to maintain a steady flow of high-quality content that resonated with her audience. She also used the content calendar to schedule her promotional campaigns, such as new course launches and special offers, ensuring that she had a well-rounded content mix that catered to her audience's diverse interests.

Next, Lisa looked for ways to automate her social media processes and save time. She researched and implemented social media management tools, such as Buffer and Later, to schedule her content in advance and automatically post it at optimal times. Lisa also utilized these tools to monitor her engagement, track her performance, and gain insights into her audience's preferences. By automating her social media processes, Lisa was able to free up more time to focus on other aspects of her growing business.

As her business continued to expand, Lisa recognized the need for additional support to manage her social media efforts. She decided to build a social media team to help her develop and execute her content strategy, engage with her audience, and track her performance. Lisa started by hiring a social media manager to oversee her channels and ensure her brand voice and messaging remained consistent. She then added a content creator to produce high-quality visuals, videos, and written content, as well as a community manager to engage with her audience and respond to inquiries.

To ensure her social media team was aligned with her goals and objectives, Lisa provided them with clear guidelines and expectations, as well as access to relevant resources and tools. She also established regular communication channels, such as weekly meetings and shared project management software, to keep everyone on track and facilitate collaboration.

As Lisa's social media team grew, she continued to invest in their professional development by providing training, resources, and opportunities to expand their skillsets. This not only helped her team stay current with the latest social media trends and best practices but also fostered a culture of continuous improvement and innovation.

By implementing a content calendar, automating processes, and building a dedicated social media team, Lisa was able to scale her social media efforts efficiently and maintain momentum as her business grew. These strategies allowed her to effectively manage her expanding online presence, continue driving results, and support the ongoing success of her online courses.

# Chapter 10: Success Stories

As you continue on your social media journey, it's essential to celebrate your successes, learn from your challenges, and consistently refine your approach to drive continuous improvement. In this final chapter, we'll discuss the importance of recognizing achievements, analyzing setbacks, and fostering a culture of learning and growth within your social media efforts.

# Recognizing and Celebrating Achievements

1. Acknowledge milestones: Celebrate milestones such as reaching a certain number of followers, achieving a specific engagement rate, or generating a set amount of leads or sales through your social media efforts.

2. Share success stories: Communicate your successes with your team, stakeholders, and audience to foster a sense of pride, accomplishment, and motivation.

3. Reward outstanding performance: Recognize and reward exceptional performance from your team members or yourself, fostering a culture of excellence and continuous improvement.

4. Reflect on lessons learned: Take time to reflect on the strategies and tactics that led to your successes and determine how you can build on those learnings to drive further growth.

# Analyzing and Learning from Challenges

1. Identify setbacks: Regularly review your social media performance to identify areas where you may have fallen short of your objectives or encountered challenges.

2. Analyze root causes: Investigate the root causes of setbacks, considering factors such as content, strategy, audience targeting, platform algorithms, and external influences.

3. Develop action plans: Create action plans to address the root causes of your challenges, including refining your strategies, adjusting your content, or seeking additional training or resources.

4. Embrace a growth mindset: Foster a growth mindset within your social media efforts, viewing challenges as opportunities to learn, grow, and improve your approach.

# Fostering a Culture of Learning and Growth

1.  Encourage experimentation: Promote a culture of experimentation within your social media efforts, allowing for the testing of new ideas, platforms, and tactics without fear of failure.
2.  Invest in professional development: Provide opportunities for yourself and your team to stay current with industry trends, best practices, and new technologies through training, events, and networking.
3.  Embrace collaboration: Encourage collaboration and knowledge-sharing within your team, leveraging the diverse skills, experiences, and perspectives of each member to drive continuous improvement.
4.  Continuously refine your approach: Regularly review and update your social media strategy, objectives, and tactics based on your successes, challenges, and learnings, ensuring that your approach remains agile, relevant, and effective.

Recognizing and celebrating your successes, learning from your challenges, and fostering a culture of learning and growth are essential components of a successful, long-term social media strategy. As you continue to navigate the dynamic world of social media, remember that persistence, adaptability, and a commitment to delivering value to your audience are key to driving results and achieving your business goals. Keep learning, stay agile, and always strive to improve, and you'll be well on your way to social media success.

---

# Case Study: Celebrating Successes and Learning from Challenges

Kevin, the founder of a digital marketing agency, wanted to foster a culture of learning and growth within his social media team. He believed that by celebrating their successes and learning from their challenges, his team would be more motivated, resilient, and adaptable in the fast-paced world of social media marketing. To achieve this, Kevin implemented regular team meetings, encouraged open communication, and provided ongoing training and development opportunities for his team members. By embracing this mindset, Kevin's agency was able to deliver exceptional results for their clients, while continuously improving their own social media skills and strategies.

To begin, Kevin established a routine of holding regular team meetings to discuss their social media efforts. These meetings provided an opportunity for team members to share their successes, challenges, and learnings, as well as brainstorm ideas for future campaigns and strategies. By creating a supportive and collaborative environment, Kevin encouraged his team to learn from both their achievements and their setbacks, fostering a growth mindset that valued continuous improvement.

In addition to team meetings, Kevin also promoted open communication within his team, encouraging them to share their thoughts, ideas, and concerns without fear of judgment or criticism. He believed that by fostering a culture of transparency and trust, his team would feel more empowered to take risks, experiment with new tactics, and learn from their experiences. This open communication also allowed Kevin to stay informed about any challenges his team was facing and provide support and guidance when needed.

To further support his team's learning and growth, Kevin invested in ongoing training and development opportunities for his team members. He provided access to online courses, webinars, workshops, and industry conferences, as well as in-house training sessions led by experienced professionals. By equipping his team with the knowledge and skills needed to excel in social media marketing, Kevin ensured that his agency remained competitive and up-to-date with the latest trends and best practices.

In addition to formal training, Kevin also encouraged his team to learn from each other by sharing their expertise, insights, and experiences. He facilitated knowledge sharing through team-building activities, mentorship programs, and cross-functional projects, creating a collaborative learning environment that fostered personal and professional growth.

Kevin understood the importance of recognizing and celebrating his team's successes, both big and small. He regularly acknowledged their accomplishments during team meetings, in one-on-one conversations, and through company-wide communications. By showing appreciation for their hard work and achievements, Kevin motivated his team to continue striving for excellence and delivering outstanding results for their clients.

At the same time, Kevin encouraged his team to view challenges as learning opportunities, rather than failures. He supported them in analyzing their setbacks, identifying areas for improvement, and developing strategies to overcome their obstacles. By embracing this mindset, his team became more resilient, adaptable, and committed to continuous learning and growth.

By promoting a culture of learning and growth within his social media team, Kevin's digital marketing agency was able to deliver exceptional results for their clients and continuously improve their own social media skills and strategies. This approach not only contributed to the success of his agency but also helped create a supportive, collaborative, and innovative work environment that attracted top talent and fostered long-term employee engagement and satisfaction.

# Conclusion

Throughout this book, we have explored various strategies, tactics, and insights that can help you build and maintain a successful social media presence for your business. From understanding your audience and setting clear objectives, to creating engaging content and leveraging advanced tactics, the journey of social media success is both exciting and challenging.

As you continue to navigate the ever-changing landscape of social media, it's essential to remember that it is a long-term commitment, requiring ongoing learning, adaptability, and a focus on delivering value to your audience. By consistently refining your approach, staying informed about industry trends, and embracing a growth mindset, you'll be well-equipped to tackle the challenges and seize the opportunities that social media presents.

Moreover, the key to long-term success in social media lies in building meaningful relationships with your audience, fostering a sense of community, and staying true to your brand values and objectives. By doing so, you'll not only achieve your social media goals but also contribute positively to your overall business growth and success.

Embrace the journey of social media success with an open mind, a willingness to learn, and a commitment to excellence. The road ahead may be filled with challenges, but with persistence, creativity, and the right strategies in place, the rewards can be immeasurable. Best of luck on your social media journey!

# Authors Bio

Dakota is an entrepreneur who started his career as an engineer in the biotech industry. After gaining valuable experience, he went on to start a number of businesses in the skincare and fitness industries to varying degrees of success. He earned his MBA in 2023, which has further equipped him with the knowledge and skills necessary to succeed in entrepreneurship.

With a passion for helping others achieve their goals, Dakota is currently embarking on a new small business venture. Through his experiences and expertise, he hopes to share what has worked for him and inspire others to pursue their own entrepreneurial dreams. In his free time, Dakota enjoys staying active and exploring new destinations around the world.

www.ingramcontent.com/pod-product-compliance
Lightning Source LLC
Chambersburg PA
CBHW070437220526
45466CB00004B/1713